Life

Ellarose Strasser

BookLeaf
Publishing

Presentation by *BookLeaf Publishing*

Web: www.bookleafpub.com

E-mail: info@bookleafpub.com

ISBN: 9789395756426

First edition 2022

DEDICATION

This is dedicated to all my friends who have helped me through my tough times.

All My Heart

I went off to college
And he stayed back at home
We said it was forever
But now I'm all alone

The distance between us
Made it rocky from the start
And even though it was hard
I loved him with all my heart

He still didn't fully trust me
From something that happened long ago
He hit me where it hurt
And I couldn't take the blow

He thought he was going to lose me
So he made his grip tighter.
It made me feel suffocated
He should've known I'm a fighter

For a whole month
He kept tightening his grip
He would get really mad
At even the slightest slip

I thought I was the problem

That I wasn't doing enough
I tried to be better for him
Especially with the little stuff

We were going downhill fast
I still loved him with all my heart
But the way things were headed
I wasn't being very smart

I thought I wasn't worthy of his love
I knew I needed to grow
Which we could've done together
But instead I let him go

Months have passed around me
He seems to have moved on
But all my heart is broken
I can't believe he's really gone

Even though I was the ane to end it
All my heart was shattered
Love is not fair
His heart seemed only slightly battered

All my heart still longs for him
All my heart still cares
All my heart still wishes
That he was still right here

Love Lessons

Have you ever been in love
Flown higher than a dove
Sent from up above
The person who fits you like a glove

The only one on earth
Who makes you know your worth
Makes you feel safer than you have since birth
Who causes you so much mirth

Everyone I thought I've loved has shown
That I'm just better off alone
Away in the wind they've flown
Another lesson from which I've grown

Dead Flowers

More flowers I am buying
Because all my friends are dying
All alone I've been crying
Telling myself just keep trying

All the pain inside
There's nowhere I can hide
I'm in an emotional mudslide
No one is on my side

All buried way down deep
My feelings begin to seep
I really want to weep
But away my tears I sweep

College Kid

Some say college is fun
But I barely see the sun
My textbooks weigh a ton
I can't wait to be done

I don't have money to spend
On every brand new trend
At a party on the weekend
I wear clothes my friends lend

I don't mind it much
All the classes and such
My friends come in clutch
They help keep me in touch

This year I'm a sophomore
Classes are no longer a bore
They are close to my academic core
Except the one about folklore

I'll continue being a scholar
It's worth every dollar
Though I wish the cost were smaller
When I graduate I'll give you a holler

Map Gap

I think he's the one
He thinks it's just for fun
Yet he still calls me hun
Even after he said "we're done"

I always think about him
So I texted on a whim
Chances of getting back together are slim
Now I'm feeling pretty grim

I sent him a snap
Saying "I like you- no cap"
He said we live across the map
That's too big of a gap

It made me feel so bad
And I'm really really sad
But I shouldn't be mad
For his honesty I should be glad

Fake Smiles

I don't know how much more of this I can take

This smile I wear everyday is fake

Worn for my friends and family's sake

There's just so much at stake

Piece of Cake

8

I wish somebody could see
What it's like to be me
Maybe they could tell me how to be
To help set me free

I lie every day
To hide the pain away
If I told someone today
They wouldn't want to stay

Some would call it fake
But they don't know what's at stake
Making sure my smile doesn't break
Is not a piece of cake

Family

For my family
I am filled with love
They are truly blessings
Sent from up above

Back when it all started
When my mom met my dad
They fell in love
And for that I'm glad

First came MJ
I was born two years later
MJ is my role model
I could never hate her

Five years after I was born
Came handsome little Jude
Being the only boy
He quickly became a ladies' dude

Yet another five years later
Josie entered the world
She always fights for her beliefs
With her little fists curled

Rita came to us
September of 2015
Always seeking attention
She just wants to be seen

Ruby being the youngest
Makes her really tough
All of her older siblings
Like to play a little rough

If I didn't mention Meghan
This poem would be amiss
Though not blood related
She is my other sis

You can probably tell
As it's pretty easy to see
I am very blessed with a family
Who means the world to me

Adventure

I've always wanted to go to space
New adventures I want to face
Travel to a different place
Away from my home base

I want to go overseas
Learn all the ways to say please
Fly around like little bees
Maybe climb a couple trees

I just have to figure out how to pay
Money does not easily come my way
But big jobs require you to stay
They don't let you travel away

Paycheck to paycheck I survive
Money I must connive
But traveling is when I thrive
It makes me feel so alive

Breaks at the Lake

12

Family vacay at the lake
For my parents mental sake
A couple days to get away
And take a little break

Falling

13

I don't know what to think
It was just a little wink
Now when I look at him
Into his eyes I sink

I just want to be seen
By his eyes so green
He seems so safe
On his shoulder I want to lean

In his arm so strong
Nothing could go wrong
I wish you were here with me
I haven't seen him in so long

Road Trip

Do you want to go on a road trip
Will buy drinks for us to sip
Bring extra clothes in case you get a rip
Let's climb a mountain try not to slip

Rock climbing in Colorado Mountains
To Tennessee to see our kins
On the way Kansas camping wins
Stop in Kentucky to empty the bins

No matter how far we go
Love in our hearts we tow
For all the family we know
And friends turned from foe

Statues

15

In a room full of people
I've never felt so alone
I wish I could be invisible
Or a statue made of stone

If I were a statue
I could watch as people go by
And just as night falls
I could watch the stars in the sky

Leaving

I can't believe you're leaving
I just kept believing
Your face I'd still be seeing
But now you're really leaving

Again I hope to meet you
Somewhere out of the blue
Maybe in time anew
You'll sneak up behind me and say boo

I'm really gonna miss
The times we shared in bliss
And the way we didn't kiss
Even with the gossip people would hiss

Nightmares

17

I've never been so tired
Yet I cannot sleep
Nightmares all around me
Into my dreams they seep

St. Stephen

I pray through St. Stephen
Through rough and even
I will always keep believin'
My side he'll never be leavin'

Catholic

19

I love being Catholic
By my side Jesus will stick
With me through thin and thick
Especially when I'm sick

I love going to adoration
It's the best thing in the whole nation
It gives my heart such elation
With Jesus it strengthens my relation

Him

I really need you to be here
For me to lay next to
So I can just cry
With my head on your shoulder

Your crumpled up tshirt
Imprisoned in my fist
Your protective arm around me
You kiss my head

Tell me everything will be okay
Tell me you'll stay

What I Want

21

All I want to do
Is wrap you in my arms
And tell you I love you
But I can't do that
Because months ago
We dropped the hat
And took a step back
But that look on your face
Seems so sad
Puts you out of place

Fake Friends

Fake friends should roast
They treat you like a host
But when you need them the most
They are a ghost

Raccoon

23

I feel like a raccoon
Always searching for food
If I don't get some soon
It will really affect my mood
Give me food by noon
I'll consider you a cool dude
I'm like a caterpillar in a cocoon
Completely changed by food